IMAGES
of America

WARSAW

Seal of Warsaw. Mermaids, symbols of Poland, flank the Congressman William A. Jones Memorial, which is surrounded by holly, an evergreen plant native to Virginia. (Courtesy of Richmond County Museum.)

On the Cover: The 20th century arrives in Warsaw along with John M. Lyell of nearby Farnham, driving what is believed to be the first automobile in Virginia's Northern Neck. Lyell was an organizer of Northern Neck State Bank. He is pictured during court day around 1905. The old Saddlery and the home of Dr. Milton Sydnor are in the background. (Courtesy of Benjamin Franklin Family Collection.)

Francene Barber, David Jett,
and Brenda Harhai on behalf of
the Richmond County Museum

ISBN 978-1-5316-4451-2

Published by Arcadia Publishing
Charleston SC, Chicago IL, Portsmouth NH, San Francisco CA

Library of Congress Control Number: 2009921315

For all general information contact Arcadia Publishing at:
Telephone 843-853-2070
Fax 843-853-0044
E-mail sales@arcadiapublishing.com
For customer service and orders:
Toll-Free 1-888-313-2665

Visit us on the Internet at www.arcadiapublishing.com

This is dedicated to the people of Warsaw, whose records, pictures, and stories have provided the information and inspiration for this book.

Contents

Acknowledgments

The authors are indebted to Richmond County Museum for the use of photographs, especially those from the Warner Collection, containing works of Albert D. Warner (1879–1912) of Warsaw, and from the Patton Collection, containing works by Forrest W. Patton (1915–1993), also of Warsaw. Additional thanks are due to the owners of private collections, including the Benjamin Franklin Family Collection and the Jamie Smith Collection of postcards. We are equally grateful to the people of Warsaw and Richmond County and surrounding areas who shared family pictures, memories, and information that enabled the history of Warsaw to come alive.

Rappahannock Indians. This Eastern Woodland tribe inhabited about 13 towns along the Rappahannock River at the time of English settlement. Anne Richardson, current chief of the Rappahannock tribe, is pictured in 1994 with Warsaw resident Ruth Brown after tribal members had built a longhouse on the courthouse green. (Courtesy of Richmond County Museum.)

INTRODUCTION

Come with us on a visit to a very small town (population 1,352 in 2008) in rural eastern Virginia, the seat of Richmond County, located on a peninsula between the Potomac River on the north and the Rappahannock River on the south. These two venerable rivers flow east into Chesapeake Bay and define our region—the historic Northern Neck, the birthplace of Washington, Madison, Monroe, and Robert E. Lee.

The village of Richmond Court House was established 6 miles inland from the Rappahannock River at the crossroads of a Native American trail and the King's Highway in 1692, when old Rappahannock County (1656) was divided to form Richmond County and Essex County, our southern neighbor across the river. In a region dominated by almost self-sufficient plantations, the town grew slowly. In 1748, at the height of Colonial Virginia's planter aristocracy, a new brick courthouse was built in the elegant Palladian style. Here county justices Landon Carter of nearby Sabine Hall and Francis Lightfoot Lee of Menokin Plantation met to discuss issues of the impending revolution against Great Britain.

Memories of the American struggle for independence still lingered in the minds of citizens who changed the village's name to Warsaw in 1832. They were expressing sympathy for the recent Polish loss of the Duchy of Warsaw, as were a number of other towns in the United States that would be called Warsaw. In 1846, the Virginia General Assembly acknowledged Warsaw as a town, but it would take another century before the town was chartered by the state. In 1948, the town initiated a mayor-and-council form of government.

With the construction of the Downing Bridge across the Rappahannock in 1927, replacing ferries that had been in operation since Colonial days, Warsaw became firmly established as the business hub of the Northern Neck. Trucks laden with corn, wheat, soybeans, and vegetables from the fields, timber from the forests, and fish, crabs, and oysters from the rivers and the bay passed through Warsaw to mainland markets, returning with needed manufactured goods.

Warsaw became a delightful and close-knit community where churches were social centers as well as places of worship. There was no shortage of entertainment. Baseball was popular, and several semiprofessionals augmented the town team. Citizens enjoyed a movie theater, bowling alley, soda shop, record store, and miniature golf course.

In 1954, the Levi Strauss Manufacturing Company opened, remaining for 46 years. Rappahannock Community College and Northern Neck Vocational Technical Center followed. In 1992, Warsaw joined Richmond County in celebrating the county's 300th birthday with six months of special events and activities. Welcome to Warsaw!

Warsaw Center. This aerial view of Warsaw taken in 1963 shows the two intersecting roads in the center of Warsaw. The east-west road corresponds to an old Native American trail that connected the Potomac and Rappahannock Rivers. The road that follows a north-south direction was mandated by the colonial government as a link between the Chesapeake Bay and the Blue Ridge Mountains. The original village that became present-day Warsaw first developed along these routes. These two roads still dissect the center of Warsaw at the junction of Richmond Road (Route 360) and Main Street (Route 3). (Courtesy of Patton Collection.)

One

County Seat and Country Town

Robert W. Lowery Municipal Building. This building was constructed in 1978 as a permanent town hall for Warsaw and was named in honor of then-Mayor Robert Lowery, an active town leader. Originally the village of Richmond Court House conducted any town business in the courthouse. This arrangement continued after 1832, when the name was changed to Warsaw, and also when it officially became a town in 1846. Even when Warsaw was chartered and incorporated in 1948, there was no official town building. For years, town business was conducted in rented space in the telephone company building on Main Street. With the completion of the town hall in 1978, the only addition has been a council chamber added in 1998. (Courtesy of Town of Warsaw.)

Bonney W. Morris. The Virginia General Assembly established Warsaw as a town in 1948. As such, Warsaw was granted the right to choose officials to govern the town. Almost immediately, the people elected a very popular and capable gentleman, Bonney Morris, to be its first mayor. Morris was well known for writing poems that highlighted the warm and humorous attributes of Warsaw and its citizens. He was honored as the poet laureate of Richmond County. (Courtesy of Mary Douglas Lawton.)

Clarence M. Bell. Bell (right) served as the mayor of Warsaw from September 1951 until August 1969. Instrumental in acquiring the land on Belle Ville Lane for the town office building, he was also active in the rescue squad. Here Clarence Bell receives a plaque in recognition of his leadership and service to Warsaw from Lowery Sanders, a town council member who also served as a president of Northern Neck State Bank. (Courtesy of Frances Bell Carter.)

MAYOR WAYNE WILLIAMS (LEFT) AND FORMER MAYOR ROBERT W. LOWERY. A dedicated leader of Warsaw, Lowery served as a councilman from July 1974 to June 2002. He was chosen by his fellow council members to be the mayor of Warsaw from July 1975 to June 1990. Lowery served in World War II as a paratrooper and was shot down over Italy. He was instrumental in helping to establish the Northern Neck Veterans of Foreign Wars (VFW) Post No. 7167. He served as treasurer, cut the grass, worked the bingo games, and was involved in the VFW scholarship program. Robert Lowery was a founding member of the Richmond County Volunteer Fire Department. He was treasurer of the department for 40 years as well as an active firefighter. (Courtesy of Town of Warsaw.)

Historic Richmond Courthouse and Drawings before Renovation. When Richmond County was created out of old Rappahannock County, the Virginia House of Burgesses in Jamestown required the new county to build a courthouse. The first courthouse stood until 1748, when Landon Carter, the son of Robert "King" Carter and a justice for Richmond County, was charged with the task of making the necessary repairs on the existing building. Rather than make repairs, Landon Carter decided to build a completely new courthouse with open arched porticoes on two sides in the Palladian style of architecture that was popular in that time. This courthouse is the third oldest in Virginia and the oldest in continuous use as a courthouse. (Above courtesy of Carroll Miller; below courtesy of Richmond County Board of Supervisors.)

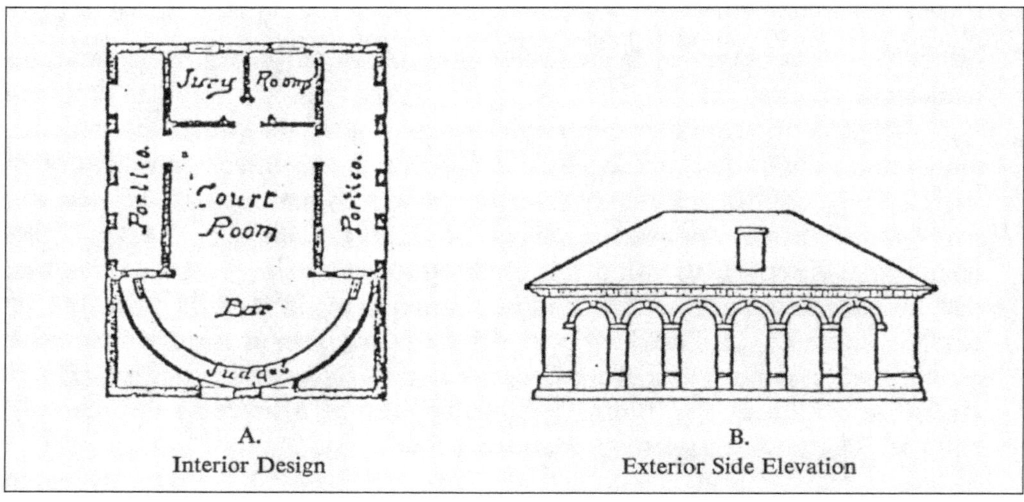

Colonial Survivor in the 20th Century. This postcard image of the courthouse from about 1950 clearly shows how the 18th-century structure of Landon Carter evolved. By 1877, it became necessary to modify the building to create more floor space. At that time, the two open-arched porticoes were enclosed, and the raised semicircular platform where the early justices sat was removed. A new entrance facing Richmond Road was added, completely reversing the original orientation of the building. A scale model of the mid-1700s courthouse is on exhibit at the Richmond County Museum. This 250-year-old edifice symbolizes both Richmond County and Warsaw. (Courtesy of Jamie Smith Collection.)

Richmond County District Court around 1910. Following the renovation of the old colonial courthouse in 1877, the district court was refurbished in the Victorian style. Portraits and busts of famous Virginians were added. (Courtesy of Jamie Smith Collection.)

OFFICE OF CLERK OF THE COURT. Col. John Tayloe III of Mount Airy was instrumental in the construction from 1816 to 1818 of the sandstone-and-stucco building. (Courtesy of Jamie Smith Collection.)

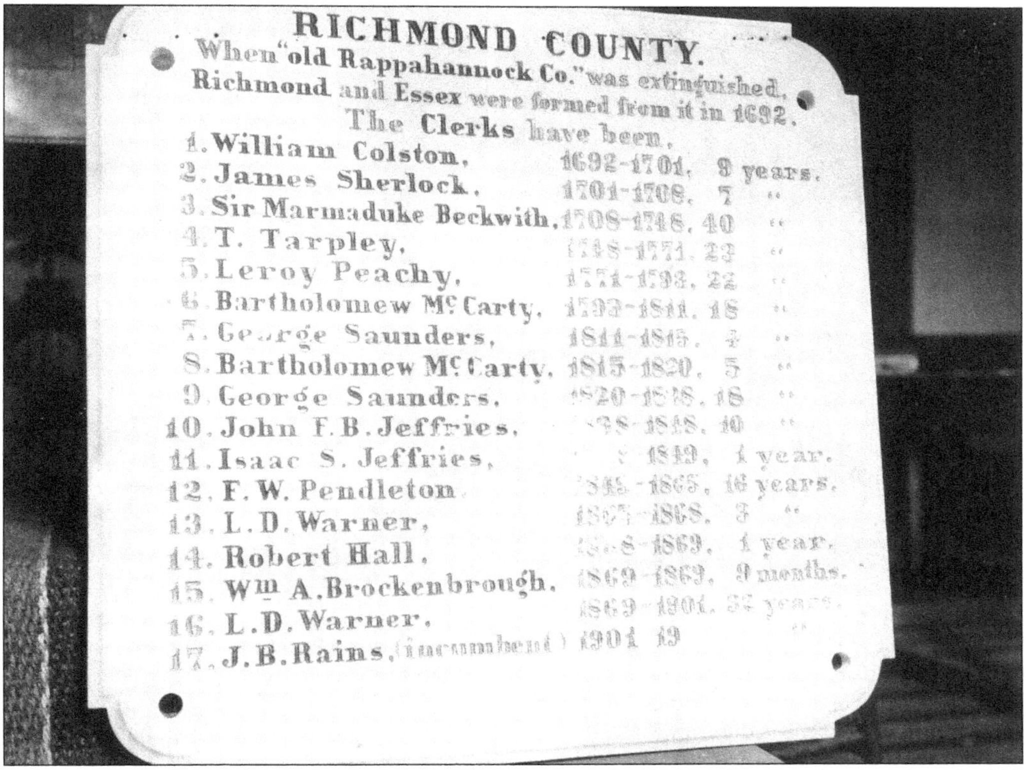

RICHMOND COUNTY CLERKS. This marble plaque was installed in the courthouse around 1908 and lists all clerks of the court up to that time. (Courtesy of Warner Collection.)

LANDON CARTER OF SABINE HALL. The son of one of the wealthiest men in the Colonies, Robert "King" Carter of neighboring Lancaster County, Landon Carter became an eminent man in his own right. He inherited and purchased large tracts of land in Richmond County where he built his Georgian-style mansion, Sabine Hall. Carter served as a justice of Richmond County and was elected to the Virginia House of Burgesses in 1752. Like his friend George Washington, Carter was a pioneer in Colonial agriculture, employing crop rotation and growing wheat, corn, and oats in addition to the cash crop of tobacco. His diary, written from 1752 to 1778, chronicles Colonial Virginia agriculture and plantation life. (Courtesy of Virginia Historical Society.)

Sabine Hall. Landon Carter built the majestic mansion called Sabine Hall in the Georgian style. The central section was constructed in the 1730s, and wings were eventually added, one in 1764 and a second in 1929. Sabine Hall is notable for its terraced gardens in six levels that slope toward the Rappahannock River. This structure has remained one of the architectural showplaces of Richmond County. (Courtesy of Carroll Miller.)

The Carter Wellfords of Sabine Hall. Pictured here are William Harrison Wellford, his wife, Ida Beverley Wellford, and their sons, Carter (right) and Hill, on the steps of their ancestral home near Warsaw about 1920. Direct descendants of Robert "King" Carter, the Carter Wellford family has lived at Sabine Hall continuously since it was constructed in the 18th century. (Courtesy of Richmond County Museum.)

Francis Lightfoot Lee. Francis Lee and his older brother, Richard Henry Lee, were the only brothers who signed the Declaration of Independence. These men had previously been part of the Westmoreland Association and signed the Leedstown Resolution in a protest against the Stamp Act in 1766. Prior to the American Revolution, Frank Lee belonged to the Committee of Correspondence, which shared ideas and strategies within the Colonies. During the American Revolution, Francis Lee served as a member of the supply committee for the Colonial army. Francis Lee married Rebecca Tayloe, and they built their home, Menokin, on land given to them by her father. Their home took a number of years to complete, and the deed was not registered until 1778. Although not very politically active after the Revolutionary War, Frank Lee was a Federalist, and according to James Madison, he was "a warm friend of the Constitution." (Courtesy of Library of Virginia.)

Old Clerk's Office. Before 1816, county clerks of Richmond County kept official papers and records in their homes. However, in 1816, Col. John Tayloe III received the commission to construct a clerk's office for Richmond County. Colonel Tayloe had the clerk's office constructed of fieldstone and stucco, materials used in his own home, Mount Airy. The clerk's office was constructed next to the existing courthouse. In 1933, Richmond County added a second room that was identical to the existing room. The clerk's office provided the facilities for the safekeeping of all county records. Currently this building houses the office of the circuit court judge. (Courtesy of Richmond County Museum.)

JOHN TAYLOE II (1722–1779). John Tayloe II was born at Old House on Rappahannock Creek in Richmond County, and like his father before him, he was a member of the county court and the Council of State. After being educated in England, he returned home and married Rebecca Plater, a daughter of Gen. George Plater of Maryland, in 1747. After their marriage, the couple began to build their home, Mount Airy, which took 10 years to complete. During the American Revolution, he supplied "Cannonball, Plank, and Pigg iron" to the Virginia Navy. Mount Airy became famous for horses that the family bred, raised, and raced, including Yorick, Jolly Roger, and Jenny Cameron. When John Tayloe died, he left 500 pounds to Lunenburg Parish for the benefit of the poor of the parish. His will stated that the Tayloe Charity Fund would be continued forever. (Courtesy of Virginia Historical Society.)

Mount Airy. When John Tayloe II and his wife, Rebecca, had been married for about a year, they began building their own home on family property on a ridge overlooking the Rappahannock River. Their home was built in the formal Palladian style, popular in English country houses of the day. The great central block of the house is flanked by matching offset wings, also called dependencies, which housed the library, bedrooms, kitchen, and servants' quarters. The materials used in the house included brown sandstone found on the Tayloe property and a contrasting trim stone of buff color from Aquia Creek near Fredericksburg. Portland stone was imported from England for the forecourt and the steps of the great hall. A deer park, a bowling green, terraced gardens, a racetrack, and a burial ground surrounded the house. The stables and remains of the orangery are still on the property. Members of the Tayloe family continue to live at Mount Airy. (Courtesy of Ernest Pickering.)

Coaching Day at Mount Airy, 1975. Col. H. Gwynne Tayloe Jr. is pictured at left. He was a descendant of Col. John Tayloe III of Mount Airy, a leader of American horse racing from 1791 to 1806. Col. John Hoomes of Bowling Green, Caroline County, collaborated with John Tayloe III to import Diomed, who was called the most important racehorse ever brought to America and is the ancestor of numerous outstanding racehorses today. (Courtesy of the *Northern Neck News*.)

Richmond County Jail. Built in 1872, the current structure contains brick from the original jail, believed to have been built in 1767. During the Colonial period, jails were built near the courthouses on the area known as courthouse green. Landon Carter, a justice in Richmond County during the pre–Revolutionary War period, was commissioned to supervise the construction of a jail in Warsaw on the land obtained from George Berrick of Belle Ville through eminent domain. The existing structure of 1872 consisted of four cells, two downstairs and two upstairs. In addition, there was a hanging chamber upstairs over the entry. Between 1872 and the 1950s, only one hanging took place in the jail. Currently this historic building is occupied by the Richmond County Museum with its exhibits and gift shop. (Courtesy of Richmond County Museum.)

Colonial Tavern at Courthouse Green. Located just north of the courthouse boundary, this building functioned as an inn for travelers for 150 years. When court was in session, county residents traveled long distances, and when cases extended for more than a day, the tavern provided meals and lodging for those citizens. The tavern did a prosperous business and was a center of activity in Richmond Court House and later in the village renamed Warsaw. This historic tavern burned to the ground in 1898. (Courtesy of Jeannette Yarborough, Richmond County Museum.)

RICHMOND COUNTY ADMINISTRATION BUILDING. The restoration of nearby Colonial Williamsburg was undertaken in the 1930s. When it became necessary in 1937 to construct an administration building for the county, plans reflected this and the Colonial courthouse next-door. (Courtesy of Richmond County Museum.)

RICHMOND COUNTY OFFICE BUILDING. By 1973, Warsaw and Richmond County had grown to the point that the existing county facilities could not accommodate the needs of the citizens. At this time, a new county office building was constructed that would include the district court and other county offices. (Courtesy of Richmond County Museum.)

District Court Building. When it became necessary to construct an additional county building, the new building was designed to complement the historic courthouse of 1748. The need for greater security combined with the need to consolidate county offices was the predominant reason for a new district court building. Opened in 2007, the new facility combines the sheriff's department, prisoner holding cells, and, of course, the premises of the district court. (Courtesy of Carroll Miller.)

Veterans Memorial. In 1988, the Veterans of Foreign Wars Post No. 7169 and its ladies auxiliary installed the Veterans Memorial in Warsaw. This bequest honors all veterans who have served to preserve freedom. The obelisk is located in the courtyard adjacent to the 1748 courthouse. There are wreath-laying and other ceremonies on patriotic holidays. Located near the memorial is a flag and flagpole that were bestowed by the students of Rappahannock High School. (Courtesy of Richmond County Museum.)

MOUNT AIRY MILL POND. The old road from Naylor's Wharf on the Rappahannock River to Warsaw ran beside the water gristmill that served Mount Airy plantation and the Warsaw area from the 18th century well into the 20th century. In the late 1800s, a store that sold boots, shoes, and other merchandise was located there. (Courtesy of Jamie Smith Collection.)

Two

Remember Warsaw!

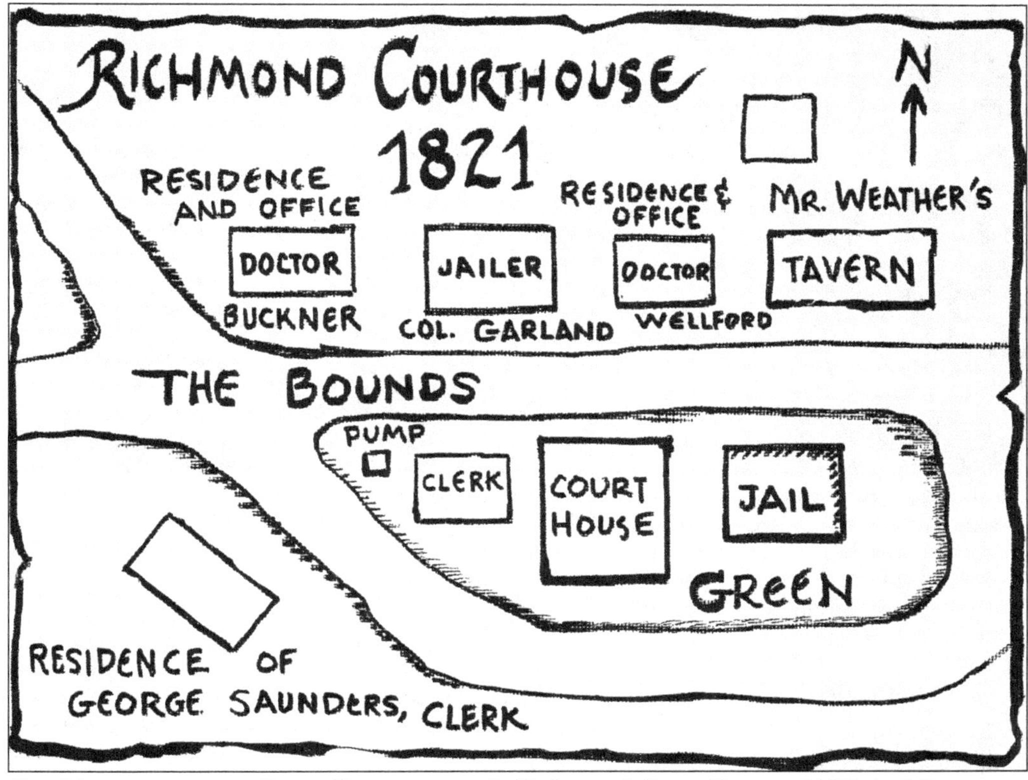

THE VILLAGE FROM AN EARLY DESCRIPTION. In Richmond Court House of 1821, buildings were clustered on and around the courthouse green. Besides the courthouse, there were the jail, the clerk's office, and a tavern. In an article in the *Northern Neck News* in 1879, the 1821 description of Warsaw stated: "The jail loomed large in the center of the public green. Between the residence of George Saunders, Clerk of the Court, on the west side of the Courthouse Green and Mr. Weather's Tavern on the east side were the residence and office of Dr. Buckner, Col. [Daniel] Garland, jailer, residence and office of Dr. [Horace] Wellford." The article also mentions Mr. Shackleford, Mr. Hall, Mr. Cook, and Mr. McSweeney as having homes on the courthouse green. Mr. Murren is referred to as a brewer and Mrs. Pursell as the proprietor of a restaurant. The sketch is an interpretation of how the village center may have looked based on the newspaper account. (Drawing by David Jett, courtesy of Richmond County Museum.)

Belle Ville. A house known as Belle Ville, with approximately 750 acres of land, became the property of George Berrick in the 1740s. Berrick then sold 300 acres to a Richmond County lawyer, Charles Beale. The land sold to Beale was mostly north of Belle Ville and going east to Totuskey Bridge. In 1749, Richmond County used eminent domain to take 2 acres from Berrick for the purpose of building a courthouse. Later, through inheritance, Belle Ville conveyed to several members of the Fauntleroy family. Eventually, Moore Fauntleroy Brockenbrough gained the land, and by 1825, he had built a new Belle Ville to replace the original home. Belle Ville remained in the Brockenbrough family until the 21st century, when it was sold. Belle Ville Lane where it connects to Main Street remains one of the original boundaries of Warsaw. (Courtesy of Warner Collection.)

The Bounds. This term referred to the boundaries of the courthouse green and the adjoining area along Richmond Road where it intersects with Main Street, forming the town center. Two acres were secured from George Berrick of Belle Ville in 1749 to build the courthouse and the jail. In 1846, the Virginia General Assembly referred to the boundaries of the village of Warsaw as "300 yards in each direction of the town pump." This picture featuring the Bounds looks west on Richmond Road. The buildings from left to right are Mallory's Store, the law office of William A. Jones, the Saddlery, the Northern Neck State Bank, and Coleman's Department Store. (Courtesy of Warner Collection.)

STILL LATER.

FALL OF WARSAW.

From the New York Courier & Enquirer of Monday.

By the British ship Arkwright which arrived last evening, from Dundee on the 24 September, we have been able to obtain from a passenger the only late paper on board—the *Dundee Courier* of the 20th, —which contains the disastrous intelligence we give below of the surrender of Warsaw to the Russians. The Captain of the Arkwright states, that when he left Dundee he had in his possession three London papers which contained a confirmation of this event, but he gave them away at the Orkney Islands, where he touched with his vessel.

☞ None of our cotemporaries have the news.

From the Dundee Courier, of Sept. 20.

FALL OF WARSAW.

This Capital has at length fallen. After two days sanguinary fighting the town surrendered by capitulation and the Russians entered Praga.

The following communication is from the Office of the London Times on the 17th.

"Official intelligence was received at Berlin, on the 11th instant of the capitulation of the city of Warsaw, on the 7th, at six P. M. after two days bloody fighting in the neighborhood during which the Russians carried by assault all the entrenchments which had been raised to protect the city."

The Polish Connection and Front Page News, 1831. News of the fall of Warsaw, Poland, to Russia may have come to Richmond Court House through the Fredericksburg newspaper, the *Virginia Herald*, arriving by steamboat or horse-drawn coach. Some residents of the village could still remember living through the American Revolution or hearing their parents' recollections of their struggle for independence from 1776 to 1783. (Courtesy of the *Virginia Herald*.)

Kazimierz Pulaski. A member of the Polish nobility, Pulaski immigrated to North America and became a general in the Continental Army during the American Revolution. He died of wounds suffered in the Battle of Savannah. (Courtesy of Richmond County Museum.)

Thaddeus Kosciusko. During the American Revolution, many Polish patriots came to the Colonies to support the cause of freedom from Great Britain. Thaddeus Kosciusko, a Polish military officer, came to the United States to join the Continental Army during the American Revolution. In 1783, the Continental Congress promoted him to the rank of brigadier general. Once he returned to Poland, Kosciusko became involved in the independence struggle going on in his own county. Following the American Revolution, Poles returned home only to find that Poland no longer existed. It had been partitioned by Russia, Austria, and Prussia and ceased to exist in 1795. When the Grand Duchy of Warsaw, created by Napoleon, revolted and failed in 1831, Russia placed rigid restrictions on the Poles. Sympathy for Poland prompted the village of Richmond Court House to officially change its name to Warsaw. Other American towns showed their sympathy in the same way. (Courtesy of Richmond County Museum.)

Early Days of a Town Called Warsaw. By 1835, the population of Warsaw had reached 100. Included in this figure were four attorneys and one physician. The structures on the courthouse green included the courthouse, the jail, and the clerk's office. Within close proximity to the courthouse were a church, two stores, one saddler, and minor dwellings. Two factories, which manufactured boots and shoes, a primary school for boys, a boarding school for girls, and two places of entertainment, existed within the town of Warsaw. The Virginia General Assembly changed the name from the village of Warsaw to the town of Warsaw in 1846. The boundaries of the town reached 300 yards in four directions from the town pump, thereby making the town a square. Although this picture was taken some years later, the center of Warsaw had changed very little from the time its name was changed in 1832. (Courtesy of Jeannette Yarborough, Richmond County Museum.)

St. John's Church (Episcopal). Constructed in 1835, St. John's replaced the ruined Colonial church of the disestablished Church of England. For many years, it was the only church in Warsaw and a place of worship for all denominations. William F. Brockenbrough of Belle Ville donated land for St. John's as well as for its old refectory, shown below. (Courtesy of Benjamin Franklin Family Collection.)

Old Rectory of St. John's Church (Episcopal), 1855. Three bishops of the Episcopal Church lived here over the years. The Reverend Beverley D. Tucker served St. John's (1873–1884) and later became bishop of southern Virginia. His son Henry St. George Tucker was bishop of Virginia and presiding bishop of the Episcopal Church. The Reverend Frederick D. Goodwin was also bishop of Virginia. (Courtesy of James C. Lamb, Richmond County Museum.)

The Garland Hotel and the Civil War Years (1861–1865). As early as 1861, Union troops occupied Warsaw and conducted forays in the vicinity. Federal officers used this ample building located just behind the courthouse as a headquarters. Built in the early 1800s, it served as a home as well as an inn and at one time was owned by Mr. and Mrs. Jim Garland. (Courtesy of Warner Collection.)

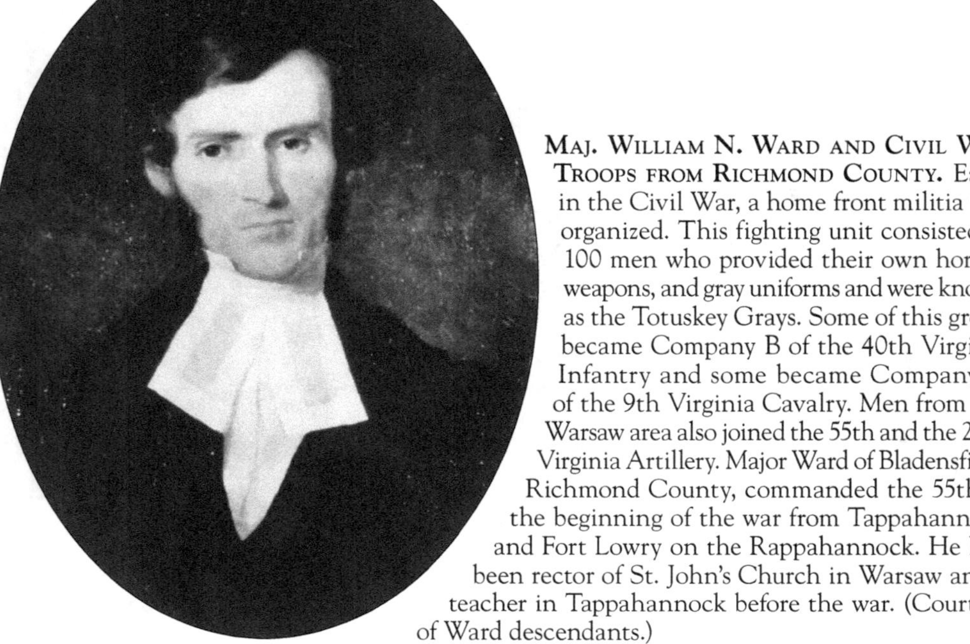

Maj. William N. Ward and Civil War Troops from Richmond County. Early in the Civil War, a home front militia was organized. This fighting unit consisted of 100 men who provided their own horses, weapons, and gray uniforms and were known as the Totuskey Grays. Some of this group became Company B of the 40th Virginia Infantry and some became Company A of the 9th Virginia Cavalry. Men from the Warsaw area also joined the 55th and the 26th Virginia Artillery. Major Ward of Bladensfield, Richmond County, commanded the 55th at the beginning of the war from Tappahannock and Fort Lowry on the Rappahannock. He had been rector of St. John's Church in Warsaw and a teacher in Tappahannock before the war. (Courtesy of Ward descendants.)

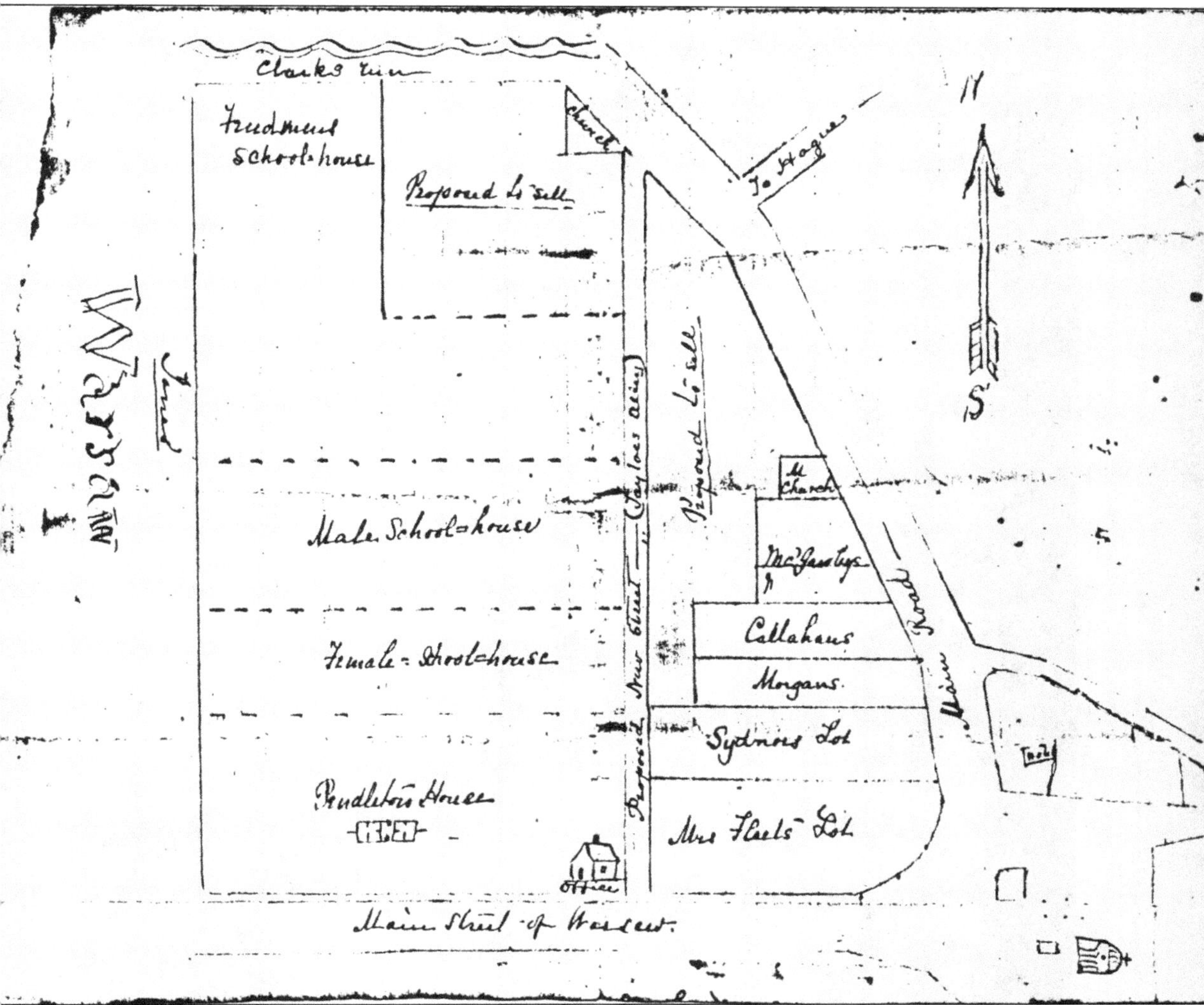

Reconstruction-Era Development Proposal. Found among papers in the attic of Mount Airy, near Warsaw, this plat was probably drawn by a member of the Tayloe family soon after the Civil War. It proposes a new street called Tayloe's Alley and lots for Freedmen's, Male, and Female Schoolhouses on land later owned by Loren D. Warner, clerk of the court. Following the Civil War, all states that had seceded and subsequently been defeated were placed under military occupation by Federal troops. Richmond County was designated a military district and placed under the direction of Colonel Hamilton. Capt. Richard Ayre replaced Hamilton, and his headquarters was located in Richmond Hill outside of Warsaw. Captain Ayre later represented Richmond County in the Virginia State Senate. Once Reconstruction ended, Warsaw again became the main commercial center for the Northern Neck. (Courtesy of Virginia Historical Society.)

The Reverend Thomas. Shortly after the Civil War in 1868, black members of Menokin Baptist Church asked for and received a letter of release so that they could start a church. The Reverend Tom Thomas, formerly a slave on the Mount Airy plantation, became the leader of this group, which founded Clarksville Baptist Church. They worshiped beneath a brush arbor on the site of the present church. In 1884, future congressman William Atkinson Jones of Warsaw sold the congregation land for $1 so it could build a church. Using its skills and talents, the group cleared the land and built the nucleus of present-day Clarksville Baptist Church. (Courtesy of Essex County Museum and Historical Society.)

Clarksville Baptist Church. The early church bears little resemblance to the present church on Menokin Road. It has been veneered in brick with brick additions, including a steeple. (Courtesy of Warner Collection.)

WARSAW UNITED METHODIST CHURCH. Long before a church was constructed, Methodists were active in Warsaw. Mrs. Pursell, who operated an eating house in 1821, was a leader in the Methodist movement. Prior to 1837, when Fereol Lemoine donated land for a church building, itinerant Methodist preachers often visited and held services in private homes. The Methodists and others also used St. John's Church as a house of worship. Finally, in 1874, the Warsaw Methodist Church was dedicated. A major addition was made to the church in 1954. When the Methodist Church and the Brethren Church joined in 1968, the name of the church changed to the Warsaw United Methodist Church. (Courtesy of Warner Collection.)

The Northern Neck News. The first newspaper in the Northern Neck was established in 1879 by a consortium of businessmen including future congressman William A. Jones of Warsaw to create a politically conservative voice that would serve the 30,000 people of the five Northern Neck counties. The first editor was Robert Hall, who served until he retired in 1891. (Courtesy of Northern Neck Historical Society.)

Northern Neck News Staff. Shown in the early 1900s is the second editor of the paper, William Y. Morgan (second from left). His brother, Frank, is the third from the left. The identity of the other two men is unknown. (Courtesy of Northern Neck Historical Society.)

William Y. Morgan. William Morgan began working at the *Northern Neck News* at the age of 16 as a printer's devil. He carried newspapers on horseback to the post office for delivery. Later he served as owner, editor, and publisher of the *Northern Neck News* for 58 years. His longevity and expertise made him a legend in Virginia newspaper history. (Courtesy of Marshall Coggin.)

W. Y. Morgan Home. Morgan's house is located on the corner of Richmond Road and Morgan Lane. As editor of the *Northern Neck News* from 1897 to 1949, "Uncle Willie" Morgan, as he was affectionately known, was instrumental in helping develop Warsaw and making it a leading community in the Northern Neck. (Courtesy of Warner Collection.)

R. Marshall Coggin. Coggin (right) was the nephew of William Y. Morgan (left) and succeeded his uncle as the owner of the *Northern Neck News* in 1949. His tenure as editor and publisher of the newspaper was a long one as he continued the legacy of his uncle. His leadership lasted for 40 years until his retirement in 1989. R. Marshall Coggin died in 2009 and was buried in St. John's Church in Warsaw. (Courtesy of the *Richmond Times Dispatch*.)

Turn-of-the-Century Court Day. The Richmond County Courthouse has remained the center of Warsaw since its erection in 1748. Court day drew hundreds of people to Warsaw, not only for court but for the conducting of all kinds of business. In this picture, the 1816 clerk's office is on the right of the courthouse in the center. The building to the left of the courthouse is thought to be Shackleford's Store, and behind it immediately to the left is the 1872 jail. The picture was taken by Albert Warner, probably from the front yard of the Warner family home. (Courtesy of Warner Collection.)

Wallace Hotel. Following the 1898 fire that destroyed the Colonial tavern, the Wallace Hotel was built, and it became a Warsaw landmark. The Wallace Hotel housed business traders, court officials, and visitors to Warsaw and the Northern Neck. A bell, located in a covered tower to the left of the building, was rung at mealtime, and the court would then recess. Individual citizens, businessmen, and people from court would meet at the Wallace Hotel for dining and to share news. (Courtesy of Warner Collection.)

L. E. MUMFORD BANK AND COLEMAN'S STORE. The L. E. Mumford Bank, which was headquartered on the Eastern Shore, opened its Warsaw bank in 1902. This was the only bank between Fredericksburg and Hampton at the time. The property where the bank was located was acquired from William A. Jones of Warsaw. In 1909, the Mumford Bank was sold to a Northern Neck consortium that then changed the name to Northern Neck State Bank. Although the bank was destroyed by fire in 1934, it was rebuilt and has been remodeled several times. To the right of Northern Neck State Bank is Coleman's Store. This store was also destroyed by fire in 1898 and then rebuilt. The stables of the Wallace Hotel appear to the right in the background. (Courtesy of Charlotte Lowery.)

Busy Day in Warsaw around 1907. This photograph depicts the courthouse bounds at the turn of the 20th century. Warsaw was the center of a county recovering from the losses of the Civil War, with an economy based on farming, fishing, and forestry. Products were shipped in and out of Warsaw from several nearby steamboat wharves. The buildings shown in the picture are as

follows, from left to right: the L. E. Mumford Bank, Coleman's Store, and the Wallace Hotel. Across the road are a small frame building thought to be Shackleford's Store, the Colonial courthouse, and the 1816 clerk's office. Doubtless it is court day, and some of the people are heading to the Wallace Hotel dining room for lunch. (Courtesy of Warner Collection.)

19th-Century Saddlery. Originally at the corner of the major intersection of the Bounds, the Saddlery was moved to its present location nearby when the road was widened. The Saddlery was constructed to make and repair saddles, trunks, bridles, bits, whips, and collars. The building features a high basement. Arches now support a brick stairway that was added after the building was moved to its present location. After ceasing to be a saddlery, the building has been a millinery shop, a draft board, a law office, a real estate office, and later a doctor's and an optometrist's office. Distortions in the picture apparently resulted from the developing process of Warsaw photographer Albert Warner. (Courtesy of Warner Collection.)

The Bounds about 1900. In this photograph, probably snapped on one of Warsaw's busy court days, people along with their horses and buggies throng the center of town. The dirt road in the background leads west to Naylor's on the Rappahannock River, about 6 miles distant. (Courtesy of Richmond County Museum.)

Looking West from the Bounds. Once referred to as Main Street, Richmond Road connected Warsaw to the Naylor's Ferry, which crossed the Rappahannock River to Tappahannock. Many whitewashed board fences lined old Main Street to keep dust and animals out of residential gardens. (Courtesy of Richmond County Museum.)

Joe Delano and Family. Sons, daughter, and grandchildren of Joe Delano gather at his farm and home on Richmond Road, heading east out of Warsaw. The purpose of the family gathering is unknown. (Courtesy of Warner Collection.)

Cobham Park Baptist Church, 1885. This church was organized about 1888, and services were held in a log schoolhouse in Cobham Park Neck. The building shown above was constructed in 1892 at the eastern town limits of Warsaw. It burned in 1933 and was replaced with another wooden structure that was torn down in 1982. Today the congregation worships in a brick church building nearby. (Courtesy of Rusty Brown.)

Sydnor House, 1890s. This elegant home was owned by Dr. A. Milton Sydnor and was located until the 1970s where the telephone company building now stands on Main Street. Dr. Sydnor was a pharmacist, but he was involved in other Warsaw businesses, particularly a tomato canning factory. (Courtesy of Warner Collection.)

Factory Scene. Vegetable canneries, especially tomato canneries, were a major industry throughout the Northern Neck from the 1870s until the 1980s. Dr. A. Milton Sydnor of Warsaw operated a tomato processing plant near the present Warsaw Shopping Center during the early 20th century. (Courtesy of Warner Collection.)

The Steamboat *Lancaster* Arriving at Wellfords Wharf near Warsaw around 1910. Warsaw's link with the outside world, bay steamers, made regularly scheduled runs from Wellfords and Naylor's on the Rappahannock, the wharves most convenient to town. Merchants in Warsaw relied on the boats to bring merchandise, usually from Baltimore. (Courtesy of Jamie Smith Collection.)

Dr. William Walter Douglas. A prominent Warsaw physician who also served as a member of the Virginia Legislature and as state medical examiner of Virginia, Dr. Douglas lived with his wife, Elizabeth Landon Chinn, in a house on property Judge Joseph William Chinn later acquired to build his home. Dr. Douglas was the father-in-law of Judge Chinn. (Courtesy of Mary Douglas Lawton and Howard W. Reisinger Jr.)

Menu Cover, Farewell Dinner for Dr. Douglas. As U.S. Consul to Bradford, England, for four years during the administration of President Grant, Dr. Douglas received a royal send-off by the Union Club in Bradford when he left England to return to Warsaw in 1877. Toasts were offered to Queen Victoria and the president at the dinner. Clear turtle soup, lobster pâté, and ragout of quails were just a few of the dishes served. (Courtesy of Mary Douglas Lawton and Howard W. Reisinger Jr.)

Snow Scene in Warsaw. Warsaw photographer Albert Warner captured this view looking west along Richmond Road after a heavy snow. (Courtesy of Warner Collection.)

Warsaw School Picnic. This picture shows students from the old Warsaw High School in 1910. Both the younger and older students participated in the outing. Note the bicycle styles and the clothing for males and females. (Courtesy of Warner Collection.)

OLD WARSAW HIGH SCHOOL, 1906–1914. The Warsaw High School of 1906 included a grammar school on the first floor and the upper grades on the top floor. The building ceased to operate as a school in 1914, when it was replaced by another facility. The building was moved closer to the center of town, where it was converted to offices and apartments. (Courtesy of Warner Collection.)

HIGH SCHOOL, WARSAW. This picture was made about 1909. The gentlemen on the top row comprised the school board, including, from left to right, Willis Morgan, Armistead N. Wellford, and a Mr. Belfield. The teachers just in front of them were a Miss Dameron, Alice Hall, and Meda Bellfield. About 90 students were present for the photograph. (Courtesy of Jean Michlem.)

Students on the Steps of Warsaw High School. Students pictured on the steps of the new Warsaw High School who have been identified include Margaret Shackleford and Betsy Mallory. (Courtesy of Richmond County Museum.)

Ada Nash, Teacher at Warsaw High School. Following the adoption of the 1869 Underwood Constitution, the Virginia General Assembly established a public school system in Virginia. At first there were one- and two-room schools staffed by a single teacher and within walking distance of most of the students. Each day began with the teacher reading a portion of scripture and leading the children in the Lord's Prayer. Teachers were paid $40 per month for a term of five months. By 1913, the school term had been extended to eight months, and the grades were extended to ninth grade. (Courtesy of Warner Collection.)

Loren Dexter Warner. Warner came to Warsaw in 1858 from Massachusetts to serve as a tutor to the children of the Chinn, Jones, and Ward families of Warsaw. His credentials included a Massachusetts law degree. He married Lucy Jeffries, the daughter of John Jeffries of the Glebe, who served as the clerk of the court in 1861. That same year, Loren Warner was arrested, most likely on the suspicion of being a Union spy. No charges were ever filed, and during Reconstruction, Loren Warner served as the clerk of the court in Richmond County. (Courtesy of Warner Collection.)

Clerk's Office. Pictured in the early 1900s, the office still retained the wooden stairs to the attic, where records were stored. Albert Warner, son of the clerk at the time, probably took the picture. (Courtesy of Warner Collection.)

L. D. Warner Home. Conveniently located across the street from the clerk's office, the Warner home was probably built in the early 1800s. It resembled farmhouses of the surrounding area and had a barn in back. The house is visible on the right in the picture of Warsaw's business section on page 101. (Sketch by Mary Anne Warner Allison; courtesy of Northern Neck Historical Society.)

Parlor of the Warner Home around 1900. A wood- or coal-burning stove was the center of this cozy Victorian sitting room, where the evening entertainment would have been conversation, reading, or perhaps piano music and singing. (Courtesy of Warner Collection.)

CHILDREN OF LOREN D. WARNER. Clerk of Court Albert Warner took this photograph in 1905. Those in the picture are the children of Loren and Lucie Jeffries Warner. On the left are Loren Jeffries Warner and, above him, Annie Yeatts Warner. In the middle are Henry Luke Warner, his daughter, Esther, and, above him, Letia Hall Warner. On the far right are Ada Warner and, above her, Elizabeth Warner Garland. (Courtesy of Warner Collection.)

ALBERT DEXTER WARNER (1879–1912). Although Albert Warner died at the age of 38, he has the distinction of being a prolific photographer of Warsaw scenes and people. His photographs capture the essence of an American small town. (Courtesy of Jean Michlem, Richmond County Museum.)

Warner School. Albert Warner established a school in Warsaw during the late 1800s on a lot near the Warner home that later became the Loudenslager tract. (Courtesy of Richmond County Board of Supervisors.)

Children in Albert Warner's School. This school preceded the public Warsaw High School and served a great many children, as the photograph indicates. Warner is the man in the center of the picture directly in front of the door. (Courtesy of Jean Michlem, Richmond County Museum.)

Warsaw Harvest Scene. In about 1907, photographer Albert Warner of Warsaw chronicled

this wheat threshing operation near town. (Courtesy of Jamie Smith Collection.)

The Warners' Horses. Like many residences in Warsaw, the Loren D. Warner home on Richmond Road had an ample barn for horses and other livestock. The identity of the man is unknown. (Courtesy of Warner Collection.)

Three

GROWING MAIN STREET

ENTERING WARSAW FROM THE WEST AROUND 1909. The new home of the Judge Joseph W. Chinn family, complete with a widow's walk on the rooftop, overlooks a sandy Main Street framed by white board fences. The place was a working farm of about 40 acres where Walter Richardson cultivated corn, wheat, tomatoes, and crimson clover and raised pigs, chickens, turkeys, ducks, cows, and horses, all for the use of the family. The Richardsons lived in a house on the property for their entire married life. Note the roof of a large barn on the property across the street. (Courtesy of Warner Collection, Mary Douglas Lawton, and Howard W. Reisinger Jr.)

Justice Joseph William Chinn. Born in Tappahannock in 1866, Judge Chinn was elected commonwealth attorney for Richmond County in 1891 and held the position for 24 years. In 1915, he became judge of the 12th Judicial Circuit Court, and in 1931, he took his seat as a justice of the Virginia Supreme Court. Prominent in Warsaw business, he was the first president of Northern Neck State Bank (1909) and president of the Northern Neck Telephone and Telegraph Company (1919). Judge Chinn died in 1936. His daughter Sally Chinn Reisinger painted this portrait, which hangs at the Supreme Court of Virginia in Richmond. (Courtesy of Library of Virginia, Mary Douglas Lawton, and Howard W. Reisinger Jr.)

Chinn House, 1908. Joseph William Chinn, a Warsaw attorney, constructed this imposing home. Chinn served as the superintendent of Richmond County Schools. He also served on the board of directors for the Mumford Bank, Warsaw's first bank, and later, he guided the direction of Northern Neck State Bank. Joseph W. Chinn was a judge of the 12th Judicial Circuit Court and a justice of the Virginia Supreme Court of Appeals. In 1968, the descendants of Judge Chinn provided the home and its surrounding land for the site of Rappahannock Community College, which opened in 1973. (Courtesy of Warner Collection.)

Chinn Children. This photograph shows three of the four children of Judge Joseph William and Sarah Fairfax Douglas Chinn. Teddy bears had become very popular with the presidency of Theodore Roosevelt. (Courtesy of Warner Collection.)

B. H. Baird House. This home owned by Benjamin H. Baird, who was born in Essex County across the Rappahannock River, typifies farmhouse architecture of the early 20th century. (Courtesy of Warner Collection.)

Shackleford Home around 1900. Seated on the front steps of their Warsaw home are, from left to right, Helen Mary Taliaferro, Ferdinand Augustine Shackleford Jr., Orin L. Shackleford, Julia Marion Cook (Mrs. Ferdinand A. Shackleford Sr.), and Ferdinand Augustine Shackleford Sr. (Courtesy of Warner Collection.)

Jeter Rains House around 1900. Rains is seated on the porch with his daughter, Helen, and son, Warren. Jeter Rains succeeded Loren D. Warner as clerk of the court of Richmond County, beginning his term of service in 1901. (Courtesy of Warner Collection.)

Congressman William A. Jones. Born in 1849, the young Jones served in the last two battles of the Civil War as a cadet at Virginia Military Institute. W. A. Jones served as the commonwealth attorney for Richmond County before being elected to represent the First District of Virginia in Congress in 1890. He served in the House of Representatives from 1890 to 1916. During his tenure in Congress, the United States fought and won the Spanish-American War. The United States received several colonies in the treaty that ended the war. Congressman Jones, as a member and later as chairman of the House Insular Affairs Committee, worked tirelessly for the cause of Philippine independence. His successful efforts culminated in the Philippine Independence Bill of 1916. Congressman Jones has often been called the George Washington of the Philippines. He died in 1918 and was buried in St. John's Churchyard in Warsaw. The people and the government of the Philippines honored him in 1926 with a memorial statue, which was placed over his grave. (Courtesy of the Jones family.)

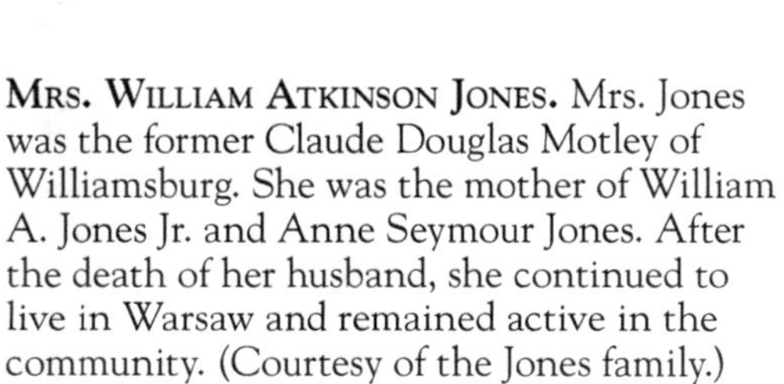

Mrs. William Atkinson Jones. Mrs. Jones was the former Claude Douglas Motley of Williamsburg. She was the mother of William A. Jones Jr. and Anne Seymour Jones. After the death of her husband, she continued to live in Warsaw and remained active in the community. (Courtesy of the Jones family.)

The Jones House, Built 1889. Attorney and farmer Thomas Jones owned the original Jones home. Jones was one of the organizers of the Totuskey Grays and served in the Civil War, rising from the rank of first sergeant to the rank of captain. Because of his Confederate service, Federal troops occupying Warsaw retaliated by burning his home. In 1889, Thomas Jones's son, William A. Jones, rebuilt the family home in Warsaw. (Courtesy of the Jones family.)

Jones Law Office. William A. Jones's law office bears a striking resemblance to his home. Both were designed by a Baltimore architect. The office stood adjacent to his home on Richmond Road and was torn down some time after his death in 1918. (Courtesy of the Jones family.)

Taft Commission, 1905. As chairman of the Insular Affairs Committee of the House of Representatives, Congressman W. A. Jones became part of a commission headed by Secretary of War William Howard Taft to visit the newly acquired Philippine Islands following the Spanish-American War. Members of the touring party included congressmen, senators, governors, cabinet members, editors, and their wives. Alice Roosevelt represented her father, the president. Their itinerary included a rail journey across the United States and travel by steamship to Hawaii,

Japan, and China. The commission was assigned to determine whether to keep the islands as a colony or a territory or to grant their independence. Congressman William Jones, a populist Democrat, was an advocate of total independence for the Philippines and authored a bill granting independence that was passed by Congress and signed by President Wilson in 1916. (Courtesy of the Jones family.)

House Insular Affairs Committee. Following the national election of 1916 and the election of Democrat Woodrow Wilson as president, William A. Jones, also a Democrat, became a powerful spokesman in the House of Representatives. With his seniority, Congressman Jones became the chairman of the House Insular Affairs Committee. In his leadership role, Congressman Jones was able to push through the bill for Philippine independence in 1916, and President Wilson then signed it. (Courtesy of the Jones family.)

Mrs. Jones Christens Ship. Mrs. William A. Jones (Claude, the third woman from left with a large bouquet of flowers) holds a bottle of champagne in readiness to dedicate a navy ship. Congressman Jones stands behind his wife. (Courtesy of the Jones family.)

JONES MEMORIAL AT ST. JOHN'S CHURCH. The monument was a gift from the people of the Philippines and the Philippine government for the dedication and commitment of Congressman William A. Jones to the fruition of Philippine independence. The memorial was unveiled on June 20, 1926, in impressive ceremonies attended by Philippine, Congressional, and Virginia officials. (Courtesy of Jamie Smith Collection.)

William Atkinson Jones Jr. Following in the footsteps of his father and grandfather, William Atkinson Jones Jr. became the third member of the family to serve Richmond County as its commonwealth attorney. Prior to this, he served the United States as an aviator in World War I. (Courtesy of the Jones family.)

SON OF MR. JONES PLEADS FOR PHILIPPINE INDEPENDENCE

There comes an epoch in the intellectual, economic and political development of every nation when further progress demands that it must stand alone and exercise, unrestricted, the right of self-government.

I believe that this period has been reached by the people of the Philippine Islands.

To deny them this right any longer is to discredit the fundamental principles of democracy, to blight the ideals and shackle the growth of a nation.

WILLIAM A. JONES

Lt. Col. William Atkinson Jones III. Following his father's legacy, Lt. Col. Bill Jones piloted an A-1H Skyraider, risking his life in a successful rescue mission in North Vietnam in 1968. He was posthumously awarded the Congressional Medal of Honor in 1970. (Courtesy of the Jones family.)

WARNER MORGAN STORE AROUND 1900. The Warner Morgan Store was located on Main Street in Warsaw and provided a wide range of merchandise for Warsaw residents as well as people living in the outlying sections of the Northern Neck. This building later became Ernest Y. Brooks's store. (Courtesy of Warner Collection.)

INTERIOR OF WARNER MORGAN STORE. Harry Warner, one of the owners, stands behind the counter. The tall man in the hat in front of him is believed to be Frank Garland. Note the saddles hanging from the columns. (Courtesy of Warner Collection.)

Baltimore Excursion, Early 1900s. Frank Morgan (standing at left) and Harry Warner (standing at right), owners of the Warner Morgan Store, pose for the camera, probably while on a trip to Baltimore via steamboat. Loren Warner is seated at right, and the other man is unidentified. (Courtesy of Warner Collection.)

Wellfords Wharf. Warsaw residents bound for Baltimore by steamer would depart from Wellfords Wharf, about 7 miles out of town. (Courtesy of Richmond County Museum.)

A Day's Hunting, 1909. Canada geese, ducks, and foxes were some of the many species of wildlife that attracted hunters to the Northern Neck. After a successful day of hunting, from left to right, Lloyd Packett, A. B. Mallory Sr., Woody Hall, and Samuel S. Hall proudly display their trophies in front of the Warsaw Post Office. At this time, the post office was located in the front yard of Loren Warner's home. (Courtesy of Warner Collection.)

In A Wheat Field near Warsaw. This fancy buggy, horse, and driver were featured on a postcard mailed in 1911. (Courtesy of Jamie Smith Collection.)

Mrs. Frank Garland Sr., 1912. Elizabeth Warner Garland was the sister of the prolific Warsaw photographer Albert Warner. Albert Warner owned and operated a cement factory behind the Warner home in Warsaw. Charles Ryland, a local attorney, later purchased this property, and it was on this land that he built his home. Albert and Elizabeth's sister, Ada Warner, at one time ran a boardinghouse in the old Warner home, which faced Route 360. (Courtesy of Warner Collection.)

Frank Garland Sr. Home, 1912. The Garlands lived in this serene house on Menokin Road, typical of the prevalent style of homes in and around Warsaw during the late 19th century and the early 20th century. (Courtesy of Warner Collection.)

Home of Mr. and Mrs. Jack Garland. An automobile sits in front of the Garland home. This picture was taken around 1912. (Courtesy of Warner Collection.)

Blacksmith Shop, Warsaw. Andrew Packett and his daughter, Floris Packett Rice, stand in front of his blacksmith shop around 1915. The shop was located at the eastern edge of Warsaw, approximately where the 7–11 store is today. Packett was offered a car dealership, but like many others, he believed that the automobile would never be practical on the Northern Neck. (Courtesy of the Packett family.)

WARSAW MOTOR CORPORATION. The Ford dealership and service station were located on Main Street in Warsaw. These buildings were located opposite Miller's Department Store. Both buildings are still being used today and are occupied by restaurants. The Northern Neck Gourmet occupies the larger building, and the smaller building is Sue's Bar and Grill. (Courtesy of Richmond County Museum.)

WARSAW FORD AGENCY. This photograph shows the exterior of the Warsaw Motor Corporation on Main Street as it looked around 1920. Although this agency enabled some residents of Warsaw to replace their horses and buggies with a Ford Model T, it was short-lived and soon became Farnham Motors at Farnham. Note the gas pump adjacent to the front steps of the building. (Courtesy of Richmond County Museum.)

Ford Service Station (Interior View). A Ford dealership opened on Main Street in Warsaw by 1920. Since cars required maintenance and service, the new facility resulted in new jobs at the dealership as well as for blacksmiths in the area. (Courtesy of Richmond County Museum.)

Mechanics at Ford Service Station on Main Street. Henry Barnes is one of the men pictured here. The Ford Model T on the right has a 1920 license plate. (Courtesy of Richmond County Museum.)

Miller's Department Store, 1916. Mr. Miller was a Fredericksburg businessman who opened this store in Warsaw in 1916. Before being destroyed by fire, this building housed both a pharmacy and a dry goods business on the first floor. It also was the site of the first hospital east of Richmond and south of Fredericksburg. The hospital occupied the second floor of the store from 1924 to 1926. The facility experienced financial difficulty and was forced to close. Several doctors continued to maintain offices on the second floor. (Courtesy of Mary Lou Dawson.)

The Second Miller's Department Store. Like the first Miller's Department Store, the second was located at the north corner of St. John's Street and Main Street. This store was built of concrete block and contained a pharmacy and a clothing store. Upstairs was a beauty shop, the office of dentist Dr. Warren Rains, and the office of lawyer Blake Newton. (Courtesy of Margaret Barnes.)

Julian Short. Short, a native of Warsaw, served in World War I. His name appears on the World War I Memorial located in the Richmond County Courthouse. Richmond County provided a total of 298 men who served in World War I. This was one of the highest numbers of any county in the country based on its population. (Courtesy of Jean Michlem.)

World War I Soldiers. Murvin Sisson, left, and a fellow soldier served their country in World War I. (Courtesy of Mary Lou Dawson.)

WARSAW BAPTIST CHURCH, 1921. On March 24, 1921, thirty members of Cobham Park Baptist Church met at the Richmond County Courthouse to organize a new church. On the charter list were the names of 81 people, but the number had increased to 105 by the end of May 1921. The original building was completed in 1923. Warsaw Baptist Church is located on Main Street across from Warsaw Methodist Church. It has continued to grow and meet the needs of its many members. (Courtesy of Jamie Smith Collection.)

WARSAW BAPTIST CHURCH PARSONAGE. This Victorian farmhouse located adjacent to Warsaw Baptist Church provides housing for its ministers. The architecture is typical of many homes that lined Main Street and Richmond Road in the post–Civil War period in Warsaw. (Courtesy of Richmond County Museum.)

Coggin Home. This was the home of Rodney Coggin on Main Street. Before electricity arrived on the Northern Neck, townspeople could hear baseball games being played on the radio thanks to Coggin. He would put his generator-operated radio in an upstairs bedroom window and turn up the volume so that passing citizens could stop and listen to the game. (Courtesy of Richmond County Museum.)

Children of Rodney Coggin. May Myers Coggin (left) and Marshall Coggin pose for the camera around 1924. Marshall Coggin became editor of the *Northern Neck News* in Warsaw. (Courtesy of Richmond County Museum.)

Warsaw High School, 1923–1962. When the new Warsaw High School was completed in 1923, the curriculum was upgraded. The school now consisted of nine grades with an eight-month term. Procedures were forced to change during the Depression, but the school remained open. Salaries and the school day were reduced, and a $5 tuition fee was required for an education. Following World War II, Warsaw High School expanded to include grades from kindergarten to 12th and extended its program to nine months. The present Rappahannock High School opened in 1962. (Courtesy of Richmond County Museum.)

Graduation Ceremony, Warsaw High School, around 1924. From left to right are Beatrice Gallagher, Ann Brooke Mallory, and two unidentified classmates. (Courtesy of Richmond County Museum.)

WARSAW RECORD SHOP, 1921. The record shop was a popular spot located where the Northern Neck Gourmet restaurant is today. From the advertisement, one can see that Columbia records were sold in the store. There was always an opportunity to play the records before deciding to purchase them. Note the World War I Victory poster still in the window. (Courtesy of Richmond County Museum.)

WARSAW THEATRE. The Great White Way came to Warsaw in 1921 when the Warsaw Theatre opened. Prior to having electricity on the Northern Neck, the theater was operated by generator. This successful business brought travelogues and short subjects to the citizens of Warsaw. The Warsaw Theatre was renovated and improved, but it burned in 1967. The theater was never replaced, and only the curb stop remains. (Courtesy of the *Northumberland Echo*, Jean Harper, photographer.)

MARCH COURT, 1927. The first court day in spring had a long tradition as an important event in Warsaw. By this time, automobiles dominate the scene, but in earlier days, it was a time to bring horses to advertise for stud services. (Courtesy of Connie Gallagher and Jeanette Yarborough.)

Downing Bridge Dedication, 1927. State senator Thomas Downing was instrumental in getting a bridge constructed to connect the Northern Neck to the Middle Peninsula and points further west. Many officials, including Gov. Harry F. Byrd, attended the opening on the bridge and drove to festivities in Warsaw and a luncheon at the Warsaw High School. (Courtesy of Richmond County Museum.)

Traffic Jam for Bridge Opening. Cars line up trying to get to the Rappahannock River to see the dedication of the Downing Bridge on February 16, 1927. Note the dirt road. (Courtesy of Richmond County Museum.)

Bridge Dedication Day, 1927. Dr. Marcus Handleman, an optometrist, president of the Warsaw Business Men's Association, and unofficial mayor of Warsaw, welcomes visitors to town. (Courtesy of Jeanette Yarborough.)

Warsaw Celebrates Bridge Opening, 1927. Crowds turned out in Warsaw to welcome the dignitaries who participated in the dedication of the Downing Bridge. This photograph shows the Saddlery on the left and the Northern Neck State Bank on the right. (Courtesy of Jeanette Yarborough.)

WARSAW BASEBALL TEAM, 1930. The famous sportscaster for the Washington Senators, Arch McDonald, hailed Warsaw as a great little baseball town. This baseball team was composed of local men from all walks of small-town life. Many of the team members were related. From left to right are (kneeling) A. J. "Juddy" Sanders, Lowery R. Sanders, Frank Yeatman Jr., Norman Settle, and T. D. Marks; (standing) manager Ike B. Hall, Berry Sanders, Dr. Warren B. Rains, Avery B. Sanders, George Washington Schools, Larry Sanders, and assistant manager Howard H. Scott. The batboy is Clarence Sanders. (Courtesy of Richmond County Museum.)

PECO AMUSEMENT PARKS, Inc.

OPENS

18 Hole Miniature Golf Course

AT WARSAW

Friday Night, August 1

6.30 TO MID-NIGHT In case of rain opening will be Saturday night same hour

Prizes awarded at 10 p. m.

Refreshments Served Free to all present

For 18 holes of play 25c

Come Everyone and bring your friends for an evening of real enjoyment, meet all your friends and see the Northern Neck's best located and most beautiful course. We shall look forward to having you with us at this opening.

MINIATURE GOLF, 1930. This ad in the *Northern Neck News* heralded the coming of a miniature golf course on the Triangle in Warsaw, located at the junction of Main Street and Menokin Road. The course drew large crowds and offered men's and women's tournaments. (Courtesy of the *Northern Neck News*.)

WARSAW BUS STATION, 1934. The courthouse, clerk's office, and the Congressman William A. Jones Memorial accompanied this picture of the terminal of the Peninsula Bus Lines that appeared in a tourist's guide to the Northern Neck. (Courtesy of Westmoreland Museum.)

VILLAGE LUNCH. Pictured is Marguerite Mahoney, daughter of Mary Hall Revere, who operated the Village Lunch during the 1920s on Warsaw's Main Street. The lunchroom was on the first floor and served businessmen of the community. The second floor was reserved for boarders. (Courtesy of Marguerite Mahoney.)

Warsaw High School Class of 1938. Pictured from left to right are (first row) Bernice Scott Bowen, Lillian France Parr, Mable Jenkins Balderson, Marguerite Revere Mahoney, Nora Hutt Shorang, Arlene Harris Lowe, Dorothy Bell Ferguson, and Betty Moore; (second row) Gladys Martria, Florence Hammond, Betty Delano Green, Madeline Franklin Waye, Eleanor France Campbell, Frances Harper, Mildred Rice France, Sara Jo Smith, and Rachael Hall; (third row) Garland Marks, Joe Packett. G. C. Sanford, John Waye, Ned Woolsey, James Schools, and Eugene France; (fourth row) James Buchannan, Miles Delano, Roland Fallon, principal Mr. Bailey, Billy Delano, Woodrow Sanders, Willis Gallagher, and Claude Hale. (Courtesy of Marguerite R. Mahoney.)

Warsaw High School. The original building of 1913 is on the right. The newer building on the left contained an auditorium and cafeteria. (Courtesy of Jamie Smith Collection.)

Northern Neck Electric Cooperative. Electricity came to the Northern Neck in 1937 with the creation of the Northern Neck Electric Cooperative. Residents and businesses could now eliminate their kerosene lamps and their generators. The first office of the cooperative was located in the Warsaw Bus Station. Next it rented a sweet potato storage shed on St. John's Street. This office remained the headquarters of the cooperative until the present office was constructed in 1995. (Courtesy of Northern Neck Electric Cooperative.)

Northern Neck Spray Truck No. 1. With the advent of the Rural Electrification Association on the Northern Neck, electricity and employment were provided to residents of the entire Northern Neck. The service crew, pictured from left to right, is Goody Hall, Milton Smith, and Marvin Neale. (Courtesy of Northern Neck Electric Cooperative.)

Northern Neck Electric Cooperative Annual Meeting. Co-op members gathered at Warsaw High School in the 1940s. Director R. E. Peed is the white-haired gentleman on the front row. (Courtesy of Northern Neck Electric Cooperative.)

BUSINESS SECTION, WARSAW. During the 1930s, the Sanitary Market and Blake's Drug Store operated at the corner of Main Street and Richmond Road. These businesses attracted many customers to downtown Warsaw. The old Saddlery has been used by lawyers, doctors, and even as a millinery shop. Blake's later became Clanton's Pharmacy and then Clement's Pharmacy. (Courtesy of Jamie Smith Collection.)

Court Day, 1930s. Court Day continued to be a very busy day in Warsaw until well after World War II. A large crowd swells the grounds of the old courthouse and clerk's office and in front of the shopping center. Vehicles seem to be headed in all directions. (Courtesy of Margaret Barnes.)

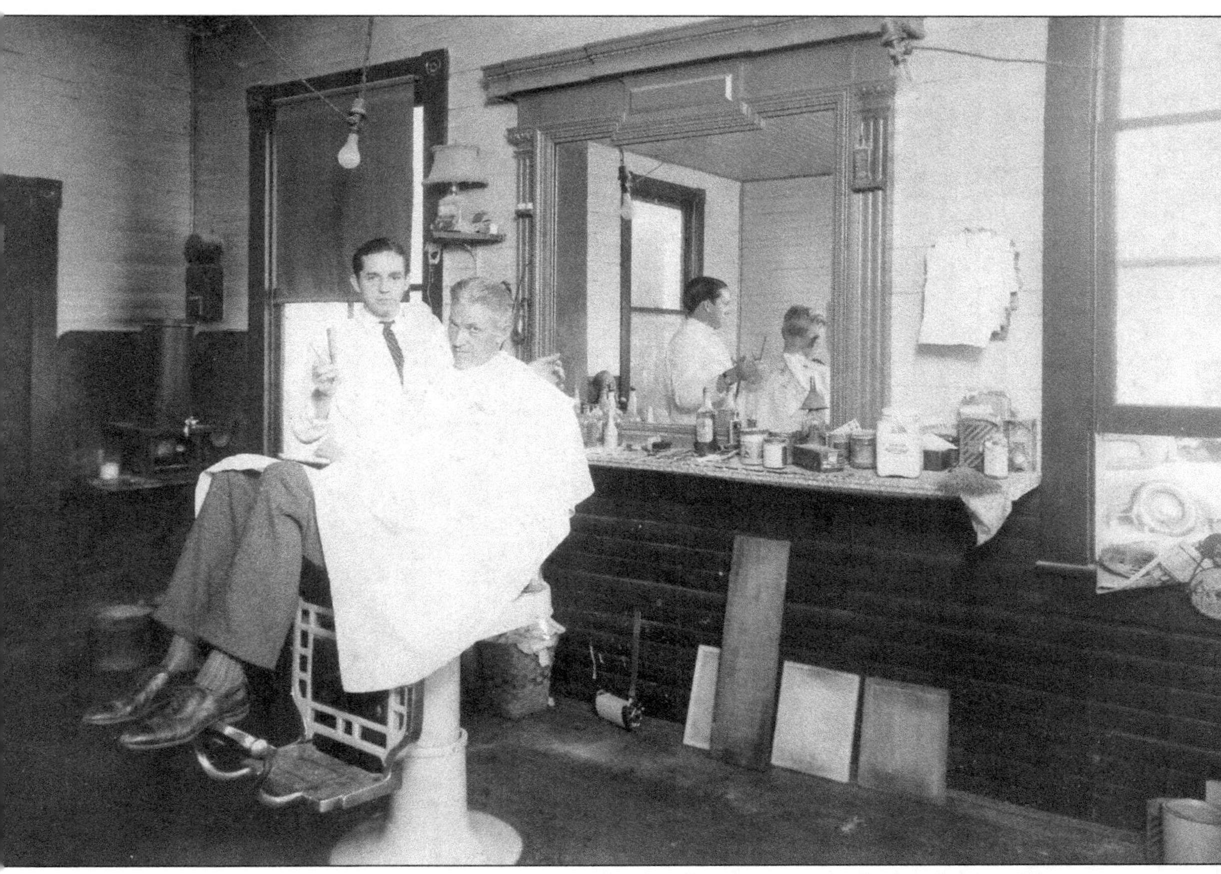

Opening Day at Sam's Barber Shop. Sam Vanlandingham operated a barbershop in Warsaw for 60 years beginning in 1927. Men regularly visited Sam's during the mid- to late-20th century for haircuts and to talk and listen to the latest news of the town. *Northern Neck News* editor R. Marshall Coggin called this barbershop a "unique Academy of Human Nature." Subjects discussed ranged from jokes, religion, and politics to "how high a certain bird dog would hold his tail when pointing quail." (Courtesy of Betty Vanlandingham Gibbs.)

WARSAW DEPARTMENT STORE. Billy Northern stands in front of his parents' store on Main Street about 1944. Northern is a well-known animal communicator today who does healing work with racehorses and other animals. (Courtesy of William and Ann Northern.)

Four

Modern Momentum

Downtown Warsaw, Early 1940s. Located near the historic courthouse was the bowling alley and Dunaway's Market in a brick building. Beyond Dunaway's was a two-story frame building that included a jewelry store and Sam's Barber Shop. From left to right on the opposite side of Richmond Road are a service station, the Loren Warner residence, a restaurant, and the Saddlery. (Courtesy of Jamie Smith Collection.)

Looking West from Warsaw Center. During the 1940s, a service station was located near the junction of Main Street and Route 360. Blake's Drug Store, with a Coca-Cola sign, was on the right next to the Sanitary Grocery. (Courtesy of Jamie Smith Collection.)

Business Section, Warsaw, around 1940. From left to right are a furniture store; an A&P grocery store; Dunaway's, a clothing store; and Franklin's Jewelers. Sam Vanlandingham's barbershop was also located in the white building on the right. (Courtesy of Jamie Smith Collection.)

Ike (Isaac) Hall, Warsaw Businessman. Hall owned and operated a grocery store on Main Street. He was a member of the board of directors for Northern Neck State Bank for almost 30 years. He served as a member of the Richmond County Board of Supervisors and later as the sheriff of Richmond County. (Courtesy of Charles Ryland.)

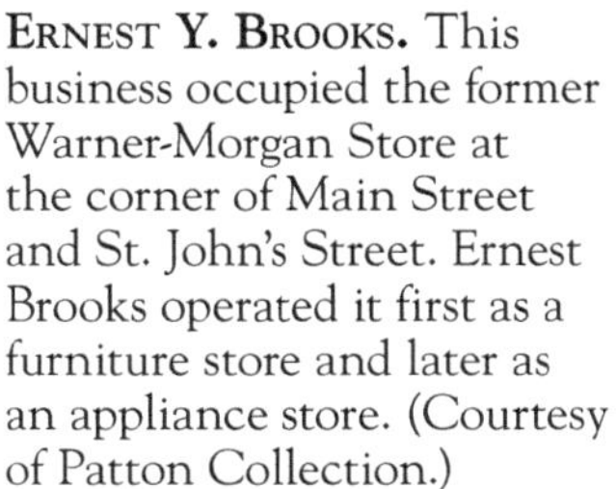

Ernest Y. Brooks. This business occupied the former Warner-Morgan Store at the corner of Main Street and St. John's Street. Ernest Brooks operated it first as a furniture store and later as an appliance store. (Courtesy of Patton Collection.)

Col. Ruby Bryant. Colonel Bryant (second from left) was the Chief of the U.S. Army Nurse Corps in World War II. This photograph shows Colonel Bryant chatting with Gen. Matthew Ridgeway (third from left) when he became commander of the Philippines. (Courtesy of Richmond County Museum.)

Lloyd Saunders. This photograph shows Saunders on active duty in the Pacific during World War II. Later Lloyd Saunders served on the Richmond County Board of Supervisors for many years. (Courtesy of Richmond County Museum.)

VFW and Ladies Auxiliary Post 7167. Participating in the visit from the traveling replica of the Vietnam Memorial were Comdr. John S. Short and members of the VFW Ladies Auxiliary. (Courtesy of VFW Auxiliary.)

The Moving Wall. In 2004, a number of local organizations helped sponsor a visit of a replica of the Vietnam Memorial in Washington, D.C., offering citizens of Warsaw and the surrounding area the opportunity to see this memorial to those who lost their lives in the Vietnam War. (Courtesy of VFW Auxiliary.)

Hinson's Lunch. For many years, this was a popular meeting place for the men of Warsaw. Here they discussed the events of Warsaw and the world. The lunchroom was located on Route 3 in the former service center of the Ford Motor Company. This lively meeting place was the subject of a poem, "Warsaw Boys at Hinson's Lunch," written by Bonney Morris, the first mayor of Warsaw. (Courtesy of Paul Welch.)

1946 BASEBALL TEAM. The Warsaw High School baseball team won the district championship on May Day, 1946. Members of the team are, from left to right, (first row) Cordell Sanford (outfield), Buddy Delano (pitcher), Boatwright Sanders (catcher), Alfred Pemberton (shortstop), W. D. Edwards (shortstop), Billy Walker (second base), and W. E. Packett (third base); (second row) Webster Sanders (first base), Howard Dishman (outfield), Stewart Dishman (outfield), Aubrey Packett (outfield), Winston Balderson (pitcher), Robert Wilkins (second base), Wilbur Hall (outfield), and Henry Seward (coach). (Courtesy of Joyce Pemberton.)

WARSAW GLIDERS BASEBALL TEAM. Frank Brown (left) and Elmer Jackson were members of the Warsaw Gliders in the 1940s. The Gliders replaced an earlier African American team called the Blue Jackets that had played in the 1930s. (Courtesy of *Close Ties*, Richmond County Intermediate School.)

Tidewater Telephone Company, Warsaw, 1954. Pictured are the original directors of the Tidewater Telephone Company, located in Warsaw. From left to right are (first row) state senator Tom Blenton, Charles Stewart, Rodney Coggin, and Sen. Robert O. Norris; (second row) Colin Chilton, John Gallagher, John Warren Cook, Judge George Walker, George Hinton, and George DeHardt. (Courtesy of Richmond County Museum.)

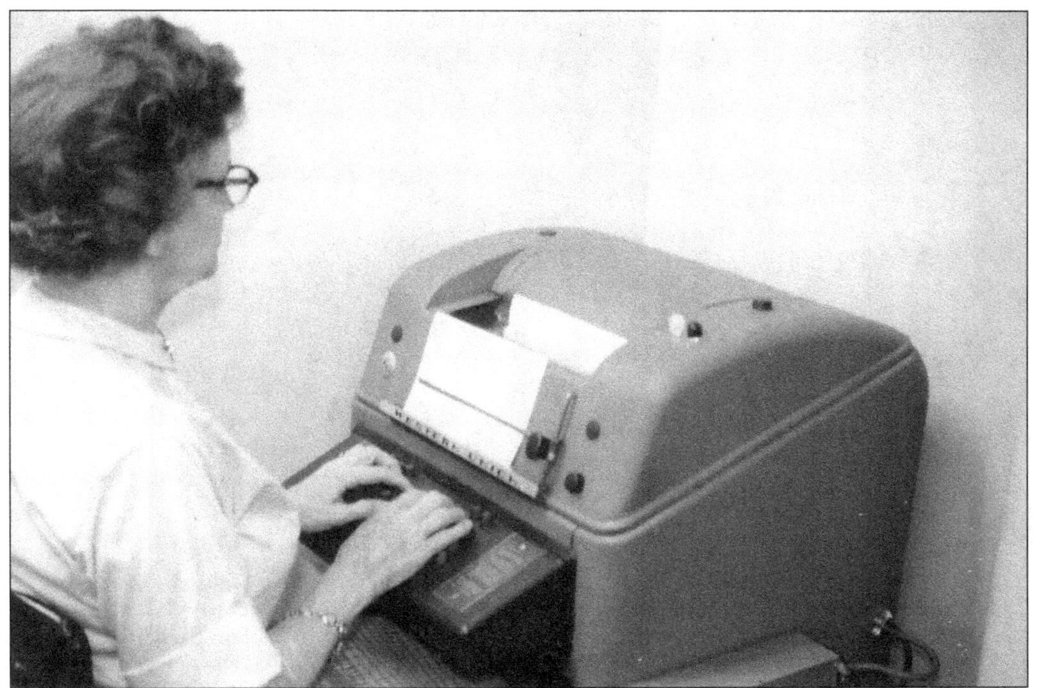

Tidewater Telephone Company, 1960s. Mary Sisson Packett is shown as a Western Union operator. Packett joined Tidewater Telephone in 1949. (Courtesy of Mary Lou Dawson.)

Tidewater Telephone Company. Shown about 1936, this building was located on Main Street (Route 3). The company was organized in 1887. (Courtesy of Richmond County Board of Supervisors and Robert B. Delano Jr.)

ENTERING TOWN ON MAIN STREET (ROUTE 3), 1951. A prosperous postwar town emerges in this photograph, with four filling stations visible along with Lowery's Grill on the left. The large building on the left was the former Warsaw School. In the center distance is the old Warner Store, which became Ernest Y. Brooks's Appliance Store. (Courtesy of Jamie Smith Collection.)

WARSAW'S WELCOME WAGON, 1954. Irving Beauchamp (left) and Annie Bruce Robertson (second from left) are shown welcoming a new resident to Warsaw. Mel Aycock is driving the 1930 Ford Model A Ford served as the welcome wagon. (Courtesy of Chris Sanders.)

Levi Strauss Plant. The Warsaw facility opened officially in 1955 just outside the town limits of Warsaw. At its height of production, the plant employed 300 workers. It was a major blow to the economy of Warsaw when the plant closed after 46 years as a Warsaw employer. (Courtesy of Patton Collection.)

Masonic Ceremony. Lodge Master Toulson, center, officiates at a note-burning ceremony when the mortgage on the lodge building in Warsaw was paid off in the early 1980s. The man to his left is Robert Bryant. (Courtesy of Patton Collection.)

Warsaw-Bauman Lodge No. 332. Located on Main Street, the Warsaw Lodge merged with the Bauman Lodge of Sharps, thus enlarging and strengthening both organizations. (Courtesy of Carroll Miller.)

NORTHERN NECK FAIR, 1955. The harness races were a popular feature of the Warsaw Fair. Pictured here is the driver, Earl Scott, receiving the winner's trophy from Fair Queen Connie Clark Dawson. Jimmy Bowen is standing at the horse's head, and the judges' stand is in the background. (Courtesy of Patton Collection.)

NORTHERN NECK FAIR. Game warden Henry Harrison (H. H.) Pitman, standing, and Frank Settle man the conservation booth at the Warsaw Fair while Mary Ellen Hinson, Maxine Shockley, and Elnora F. Campbell look on. (Courtesy of Forrest Patton Collection.)

CLEMENT'S PHARMACY. Warsaw High School students posed for an advertising photograph that appeared in their yearbook in 1963. The drugstore was located on Richmond Road close to the intersection of Route 3. Students pictured include Mary Grace Fones, Pat Packett Pugh, Shirley Wheeler, Pat Barton, Brad Lowery, Michael Mundie, Donna Sandy, and Mac Lowery. (Courtesy of Richmond County High School.)

Looking West from Warsaw Center. This picture was taken in the late 1950s and shows the area just west of the intersection between Main Street and Richmond Road. (Courtesy of Richmond County Museum.)

Ben Franklin Variety Store Opens. Mayor Clarence Bell cuts the ribbon while store owner H. L. Horn watches. Representatives of the Ben Franklin chain participated in the ribbon cutting ceremony. For many years, Ben Franklin operated as a department store, selling household items and notions. The store was located in the Warsaw Shopping Center in "The Bottom" on Richmond Road. (Courtesy of William Northern and the *Northern Neck News*.)

Welcome Home Parade for Yankee Pitcher Jim Coates. Majorettes and a marching band pass in front of Northern Neck State Bank and the Wallace Hotel in October 1961. The New York Yankees had won the World Series that year. During Coates's 20-year career in baseball, he also played for the Washington Senators, Cincinnati Reds, and California Angels. Coates was an All-Star and pitched in two winning World Series with the Yankees. (Courtesy of the *Northern Neck News.*)

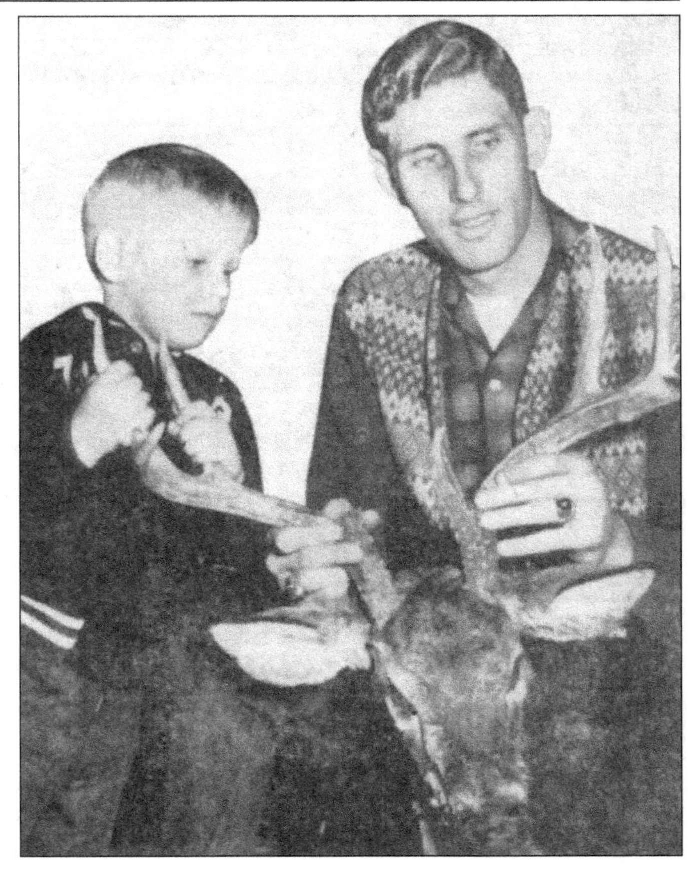

Jim Coates and Son Jimmy. An avid hunter of deer and quail, Coates liked to spend off-seasons back in the Northern Neck, where he bagged this nine-point buck in December of 1961. (Courtesy of the *Richmond Times Dispatch.*)

Warsaw Pony League. In 1962, after an undefeated season, the Warsaw Pony League team went on to win the championship. The leading hitter on the team was A. D. Davis with a batting average of .444. From left to right are (first row) Ed Smith, Billy Clark, Dickie Brooks, Richard Baker, Lannie Williams, and Donnie Smith; (second row) Ben Franklin, Chris Sanders, Larry Altaffer, Roger Hanks, Brad Lowery, and Ryland Yeatman; (third row) T. D. Marks, coach Mac Lowery, Johnny Gray, Leslie Hammack, Arnold Smith, A. D. Davis, and coach Buddy Delano. (Courtesy of Patton Collection.)

The Buggy Is Back. Wellford Courtney shows off his horse and buggy in front of the post office building on Main Street in 1963. He participated in parades in Warsaw. (Courtesy of Mary Lou Dawson.)

RAPPAHANNOCK HIGH SCHOOL, 1962. Warsaw High School and Farnham High School were consolidated into Rappahannock High School in 1962. The high school was now centrally located in the middle of Richmond County. (Courtesy of the *Northern Neck News.*)

RICHMOND COUNTY PRINCIPALS AND SCHOOL BOARD MEMBERS AROUND 1962. The two men in front are Blake T. Newton, left, superintendent of schools from 1913 to 1954, and James N. Stover, superintendent of schools from 1969 to 1985. The woman second from left in the white hat is Madeline Norman Edwards of Farnham. Ninth from the left is Robert T. Ryland, superintendent of schools of Richmond County from 1954 to 1966. The man on the far right is William Acree, principal of Farnham High School, and to the left of him is Leslie Hodges, principal of Warsaw High School for many years. (Courtesy of Patton Collection.)

Forrest W. Patton. Patton was born in Ohio in 1915 and came to Virginia in 1945 to work as an extension forester for Virginia Polytechnic Institute in Blacksburg. In 1956, he moved to Warsaw. Photography was his avocation, and he captured many aspects of life in the town and rural Richmond County, including weddings and visits of state governors. Patton's love of the Northern Neck of Virginia combined with his notable talent with the camera produces a vivid record of life here in the late 20th century. He is shown with bags of pinecones harvested for seed. (Courtesy of Patton Collection.)

Forrest W. Patton, 1960s. Patton worked as an area forester for Chesapeake Corporation, a large paper-manufacturing company with a plant in West Point, Virginia. He is shown distributing 100 pine seedlings to Warsaw school children to encourage reforestation. (Courtesy of Patton Collection.)

Downing Bridges, 1963. In 1927, the original Downing Bridge was built to connect the Northern Neck and Middle Peninsula. This bridge replaced a ferry system that had existed since Colonial days. The new Downing Bridge was constructed in 1963 to eliminate the drawbridge component. (Courtesy of Patton Collection)

Rockwell Bryant's Gas Station. This business was located at Main Street and Belle Ville Lane where the Warsaw Office Supplies is currently located. Pictured are Rockwell Bryant on the left and Irving "Happy" Barnes on the right around 1960. (Courtesy of Patricia Shumaker.)

Northern Neck News. Without a railroad, bridges, or a newspaper, the Northern Neck remained very isolated in the late 1800s. Newspapers from Fredericksburg and Williamsburg were rare and often untimely in their arrival. After 1879, with the creation of the *Northern Neck News*, the citizens of the Northern Neck were provided with relevant and timely news articles. Currently the newspaper is owned and operated by Lakeway Publishing Company. (Courtesy of Sabrina Prescott Barber.)

Rappahannock Community College, 1973. In 1964, the Northern Neck Planning Commission approved the idea of a technical college to serve the Northern Neck. The Rappahannock Community College was built on land donated by the Chinn family. When the college opened in 1973, it became the north campus, and the Saluda facility became the south campus of the same institution. (Courtesy of Sabrina Prescott Barber.)

Bicentennial Parade, 1976. Grand marshal and U.S. senator John Warner (right) was joined by U.S. representative Thomas Downing as honorary grand marshal in the Richmond County Bicentennial Celebration, held in Warsaw. (Courtesy of Patton Collection.)

MUSEUM OPENING, 1992. Richmond County Museum began as part of the Richmond County Tercentennial Celebration. It was first housed in the old clerk's office. (Courtesy of Richmond County Museum.)

THE BOUNDS, LOOKING WEST IN 2005. This view of Richmond Road suggests the movement of business and residences away from the center or Bounds (courthouse boundaries and adjoining area) of the town and outward into subdivisions and shopping centers that began in the late 20th century. (Courtesy of Richmond County Museum.)

Rededication of the Jones Memorial, 2006. Congressman Robert Wittman, representing Virginia's 1st Congressional District (fourth from left), joins with Philippine officials and the family of Congressman William Atkinson Jones, who held the same seat and authored the Philippine Independence Bill, for a ceremony marking an extensive restoration of the 1926 monument. (Courtesy of Carroll Miller.)

NORTHERN NECK STATE BANK, 1970. In 2009, the bank celebrated 100 years of service to Warsaw and the Northern Neck. (Courtesy of Patton Collection.)

VICTORY BAPTIST CHURCH. Located on Richmond Road at the western end of Warsaw, this church was officially formed in 1975 and acquired land from Herbert Delano, a dairy farmer, for its building. Dr. Ben Wharton served as the first pastor and left Victory in 2002 after 26 years of service. That year, Todd Brown, the current pastor, took over. Over the years, the church has sponsored a radio ministry and the Berachah Christian Academy. (Courtesy of Todd Brown, Victory Baptist Church, and Richmond County Museum.)

Courthouse Complex, 2006. The 1748 courthouse is visible in the center. (Courtesy of John Slusser, Town of Warsaw.)

Main Street, Warsaw. This aerial view focuses on Main Street from the Route 360 intersection looking north toward Route 3. (Courtesy of John Slusser, Town of Warsaw.)

www.ingramcontent.com/pod-product-compliance
Lightning Source LLC
LaVergne TN
LVHW081558100826
845153LV00004B/411

9781531644512